☆ WEAPONS OF WAR
ARTILLERY
1945 TO TODAY

A⁺

Smart Apple Media

© 2015 Smart Apple Media, an imprint of Black Rabbit Books
P.O. Box 3263, Mankato, Minnesota, 56002
www.blackrabbitbooks.com

Published by arrangement with Amber Books

Contributing authors: Chris Chant, Steve Crawford, Martin J. Dougherty,
Ian Hogg, Robert Jackson, Chris McNab, Michael Sharpe, Philip Trewhitt

Special thanks to series consultant Dr. Steve Potts

Photo credits: Art-Tech/Aerospace, Cody Images, Corbis, U.S. Department of Defense

Illustrations: © Art-Tech/Aerospace

Library of Congress Cataloging-in-Publication Data

Hogg, Ian V., 1926-
Artillery : 1945 to today / Ian Hogg.
pages cm. — (Weapons of war)
Includes index.
ISBN 978-1-62588-040-6
1. Artillery — Catalogs. 2. Artillery — History —2 0th century. 3. Artillery — History — 21st
century. I. Title.
UF145.H5673 2015
623.4'12--dc23
                              2013033330

Printed in the United States at Corporate Graphics,
North Mankato, Minnesota
PO1649
2-2014

9 8 7 6 5 4 3 2 1

CONTENTS

Introduction

Big gun power

Artillery dominated the battlefield for much of the 20th century and will be an influence throughout the 21st century, too.

For centuries, artillery has demonstrated the capability to change the course of history. Its evolution through modern times has maintained the potential to dominate the battlefield in a tactical sense and to bring nations to the brink of destruction or the negotiating table as an instrument of strategic diplomacy. Conventional, nuclear, biological and chemical weapons, guided munitions, and smart systems continue to keep artillery relevant during

the conflicts of the twenty-first century. Although some have theorized that the days are over when artillery will dominate the battlefield landscape, observing the nature of combat since the end of World War II results in a different conclusion. Artillery has not only exerted influence on the ground; it has stretched into the sky and beyond the horizon.

The end of World War II marked a watershed in modern history. Weapons

D-30 122MM: see page 29

L118 105MM: see page 37

WEAPONS OF WAR

systems were modernized, upgraded, and invented at an astonishing rate. While the repercussions of the war itself are still being felt on a global scale, these advances in arms and armament have influenced military actions during the last half-century and will continue to do so in the future. The idea and application of artillery was altered perhaps more than any other weapon type as a result of the massive conflict of 1939–45.

FLASH AND FIRE

With a cloud of smoke and flame, hurtling towards the stratosphere, the ballistic missile came into being during World War II. This advancement shaped the development and influence of artillery on the course of political and military events far beyond what most people realize. Artillery, therefore, is at center stage in modern military thinking. Civilian leaders and military commanders must consider its potential impact on the outcome of battle more so than ever before. The introduction of artillery shells tipped with nuclear warheads; air defense missiles which control the skies for hundreds of miles around them; anti-tank projectiles capable of defeating the most advanced armored vehicles; and intercontinental ballistic missiles packing such devastating power that they could destroy civilization

FH-70 155MM: see page 35

G-5 155MM: see page 34

as we know it in a matter of minutes — all give reason for analysts and observers to pause.

THE SEARCH FOR GREATER ACCURACY AND POWER

Once the engineers and scientists had exhausted nuclear weapon development, they tried their skills on artillery. There was no fundamental change in the principles: guns were still tubes closed at one end in which a charge of powder was burned to blow a projectile out of the other end. What changed were the methods; computers were introduced to do ballistic calculations which had been done by pencil, paper, and logarithms, which meant that they could be done to a far greater level of accuracy and far more quickly. Fuses used electronic chips to perform timing and switching functions previously done by coarse mechanical methods. Gyro-compasses, infrared, lasers, and radar could be used, together with satellites, to fix the position of the gun accurately. Pilotless aircraft carrying infrared or television cameras and other sophisticated methods of surveillance could provide information for the guns to a greater distance inside enemy lines than

M109 SP GUN: see page 38

a observer with binoculars could hope to see. All of which gave the guns far more data than ever before, leading to more accurate fire and faster response times.

Engineers and scientists now turned to guns themselves. During World War II a great deal of basic research into gun manufacture, shell design, and propellant chemistry had taken place; much of it unfinished and abandoned when the war ended. New technology now provided answers which had not been apparent in 1945. Gun design improved, producing stronger and lighter guns; shell design improvements brought projectiles with stub wings and hollow tails, reducing drag and increasing range. Since faster response by "our" artillery probably meant faster retaliation by "their" artillery, the self-propelled gun took on new importance, while the standard towed gun was now endowed with auxiliary propulsion so that it could "shoot and scoot" under its own power to some hiding

PANZERHAUBITZE 2000: see page 46

WEAPONS OF WAR

place before retaliatory fire arrived and without having to wait for its tractor.

THE MISSILE

By this time artillery had embraced the missile; by the early 1960s heavy anti-aircraft artillery was almost entirely replaced by missiles. Monster long-range guns were a thing of the past, replaced by the intercontinental ballistic missile which could span half the globe or the tactical missile. Air defense against low-flying ground attackers remained largely the business of light automatic guns, given a new lease on life by electro-optical sights connected to electronic computers, combinations which could measure a target's speed and course and predict with great accuracy where it would be when the shell got there.

However, science and engineering ingenuity work both ways; as well as producing new and better guns, they can produce new and more difficult targets and counter-measures. The helicopter may seem to be an easy target, but it is far more difficult to hit than it looks, and some clever technology has had to be called upon to counter it. A supersonic missile flying a few feet above the ground is a lethal threat: how can you stop it? How do you camouflage your gun so that infra-red sensors cannot detect it? In the course of a century, then, the use of artillery has evolved from black powder and non-recoil carriages, controlled by a man sitting on a horse and using a pair of field-glasses and a wet finger, to guns which can fire 20 or 30 miles and hit targets they cannot see with shells that can steer themselves to the target. From rockets which were no more than glorified fireworks, to missiles which fly 5,000 miles and then spew out independent warheads which fly off each to its own particular target. From anti-balloon cannons to automatic Gatling guns which throw up to 6,000 20mm shells into the air in a minute.

ON THE MOVE

Lightweight, airmobile guns provide the power behind the deployment of light infantry formations which are capable of rapid movement. In contrast, the movement of tanks and armored vehicles may be a time-consuming task. Therefore, when time is of the essence, it is artillery that is adapted to support an armed intervention on the most efficient and mobile basis.

While artillery remains a principal component of combined arms in both offensive and defensive scenarios, it does provide the commander with the option of a single response. Artillery may fire from a distance without the necessity of engaging troops or air support.

On the offensive, artillery may be used to blast a gap in an opposing line or to suppress enemy fire against advancing troops, protecting flanks for formations on the move, and shifting the campaign forward at a pace that is faster than relying on vehicles, particularly when the vehicles are required to deploy in difficult terrain or a confined space. On the defensive, meanwhile, artillery is a game changer when brought to bear against an enemy counterattack or in the defense of fixed positions. In counter-battery operations, it prevents enemy artillery from hitting marshalling yards or command centers. Gaining the upper hand on the battlefield allows freedom of movement, and artillery establishes the base from which other ground operations may exploit the enemy's weakness.

Advocates of both rocket and towed artillery point out that each has become lighter and more battlefield-efficient than its predecessors, while even lighter self-propelled artillery is in some cases fit for rapid ground deployment. One component of firepower with favorable mobility involves the introduction of lightweight titanium in the construction of field artillery.

ASTROS: see page 23

percent lighter at just over 9,000 pounds (4,000 kg) than the M198 towed howitzer which it is designated to replace. With an effective striking arc of up to 25 miles (40 km) with extended-range ammunition, the M777 entered service in 2005 and has equipped units of the US, Canadian, and Australian armed forces.

Its airmobile transport capability has made the M777 an ideal heavy support weapon during the wars in Iraq and Afghanistan, equipping the artillery batteries of many light infantry and airborne units. During one engagement against Taliban forces in Afghanistan, a pair of Canadian M777s inflicted serious casualties on the enemy while firing only a few rounds. Among the sophisticated ammunition used by modern artillery systems are high-explosive fragmentation and improved conventional munitions (ICMs), which are often used for area bombardment; anti-personnel flechette projectiles; HEAT (high-explosive anti-tank) munitions; smoke shells; cluster munitions which scatter smaller bomblets across the battlefield; and ADHPM (artillery-delivered high precision munitions).

The M982 Excalibur artillery shell, developed by US defense contractor Raytheon Missile Systems and the Swedish BAE Systems Bofors, has been

MLRS: see page 43

EXPLOSIVE

Strong and durable, titanium has replaced heavier materials in the construction of the M777 155mm howitzer. The introduction of the material was a key element of the response of the Global Combat Systems division of defense contractor BAE Systems to the demands of modern ground combat.

Designated originally as an ultralight field howitzer, the M777 is roughly 42

battle-tested with outstanding results. Fired from such platforms as the M777 155mm field howitzer and the 155mm M109A6 Paladin self-propelled howitzer during action in Iraq, the Excalibur is an extended-range shell which utilizes folding fins to assist in gliding to its target. Precision is achieved through a GPS system which guides the shell with astonishing accuracy.

Reports from Iraq indicate that the Excalibur shell was utilized in the summer of 2007 with 92 percent of its rounds landing within 13 feet (4 m) of the intended target. The use of Excalibur not only improves the results of the artillery fire and allows it to function in a close-support role but also limits collateral damage in populated areas.

ANTI-TANK TECH

In response to a generation of improved main battle tanks, including the Russian T-90, Israeli Merkava, German Leopard 2, and US M1A1 Abrams, sophisticated anti-tank missiles have been developed. The Russian 9M133 Kornet was reported in the hands of Hezbollah militants during the Israeli invasion of southern Lebanon in 2006, and its shaped HEAT charge is capable of penetrating up to 47 inches (1,190 mm) of armor protection. During one reported engagement, 11 Merkava tanks were damaged by Hezbollah fighters

SS-1 SCUD B: see page 54

MIM-104 PATRIOT: see page 41

armed with the Kornet, which usually has a two-person crew. The missile is also effective against low-flying aircraft, and has a range of 5,468 yards (5,000 m).

In 2004, the Russian Ground Forces also deployed the AT-15 Springer anti-tank missile, which is officially known as the 9M123. Mounted atop the 9P157-2 tank-destroyer chassis, which is adapted from that of the BMP-3 fighting vehicle, the AT-15 tracks targets with radar and locks on with an onboard laser.

Although the United States cancelled its LOSAT (Line of Sight Anti-Tank) program, the Compact Kinetic Energy Missile (CKEM) was tested extensively, including a live-fire event which occurred in 2006 against a stationary T-72 tank. The CKEM delivers a kinetic energy penetrator warhead at a speed of up to Mach 6.5. The missile weighs 99 pounds (45 kg) and has an estimated range of 10,936 yards (10,000 m).

SA-7 GRAIL: see page 51

ZSU-23: see page 59

WEAPONS OF WAR

FIM-92 STINGER: see page 30

MODERN ERA

During the modern era, technology and ingenuity — and indeed the flow of armed conflict itself — have not altered the conclusion that artillery is a deciding factor in the course of a fight. Prolonged air bombardment can weaken the enemy's will to resist; however, the 1991 Gulf War and Operation Iraqi Freedom which followed a decade later were prosecuted to final victory by troops advancing on the ground, preceded by sustained artillery bombardment and accompanied by towed, self-propelled, air-defense and anti-tank artillery capable of engaging and defeating a mechanized and determined enemy.

While the complexity of artillery has increased substantially since 1945, the capabilities of artillery have grown

PERSHING: see page 47

exponentially. Not only is its destructive capacity unequaled in military history, but artillery is also able to go more places, engage a greater variety of targets, and displace these targets more quickly than ever before. The introduction of lighter materials facilitates airlift and rapid deployment. The refinement of the laser, sophisticated radar, and integrated fire-control systems results in astonishing accuracy. The well-trained and motivated soldier manipulates an offensive and defensive system of awesome complexity and immense destructive force. The future of the entire planet is placed in the hands of a relative few.

Considering a forward focus, the future of artillery as a tactical weapon seems assured, while its strategic implications are unlikely to diminish. From high-tech futuristic engagements between modern armies to the suppression of terrorist guerrillas ensconced in mountainous hideaways, artillery exerts its force today and will do so in the future with saturation and precision. In truth, modern artillery has assumed an authoritative role in both peace and war.

MINUTEMAN: see page 36

AS-90

Vickers Armstrong, while carrying out sub-contract work on the failed SP70 project, could see the defects in the design and thus set about preparing an improved version of their own. At first it was developed as a turret and gun unit which could be dropped into a suitable tank hull in order to produce an SP gun, but as SP70 became more impractical, a complete vehicle was developed. When SP70 was aborted, the British had the choice between the latest version of the US M109, or the AS-90. The former was, by this time, stretching its design to the limits, whereas the latter was new and had a long upgrade life ahead of it. It was selected and went into service in 1993. It mounts a 39-caliber howitzer, but is capable of mounting 45- and 52-caliber weapons.

SPECIFICATIONS

COUNTRY OF ORIGIN: United Kingdom
TYPE: Self-propelled artillery
WEIGHT: 44.29 tons (45,000 kg)
PERFORMANCE: maximum road speed 34 mph (55 km/h); fording 5 feet (1.50 m); vertical obstacle 35 inches (0.88 m); trench 9 feet 2 inches (2.8 m)
POWERPLANT: one Cummins V-8 diesel developing 660 hp (492 kW) at 2800 rpm
ARMAMENT: one 155 mm howitzer
ARMOR: 17 mm maximum
DIMENSIONS: length 23 feet 8 inches (7.20 m); width 11 feet 2 inches (3.40 m); height: 9 feet 10 inches (3 m)
CREW: 5
RANGE: 150 miles (240 km)

ASTROS 2

ASTROS stands for Artillery Saturation Rocket System, which was developed in Brazil, primarily for export, in the early 1980s. The whole system incorporates three different calibers of rocket (127 mm, 180 mm, and 300 mm) and three corresponding launchers (32, 16, and 4 tubes respectively), controlled by a Contraves "Fieldguard" radar and computing system. The system has been adopted by the Brazilian Army and has also been exported. All launchers are mounted on 6x6 armored trucks of various sizes, and there are also armored resupply vehicles. The rockets are solid fueled, with HE-Fragmentation warheads, and the SS-60 300 mm rocket also has a bomblet warhead carrying 65 dual-purpose anti-tank/anti-personnel sub-munitions. The details below are for the SS-40 system.

SPECIFICATIONS

COUNTRY OF ORIGIN: Brazil
TYPE: Free-flight rockets
CALIBER: 180 mm
MAXIMUM RANGE: 17,500 yards (16,000 m)
MAXIMUM VELOCITY: not known
WEIGHT OF ROCKET: 335 pounds (152 kg)
LENGTH OF ROCKET: 13.77 feet (4.20 m.)
LAUNCHER WEIGHT: not known
WARHEAD: HE-Fragmentation

Bloodhound

Bloodhound was the static version of Thunderbird, the mobile air defense equipment. Part of the Air Defenses of the United Kingdom, it was deployed in some numbers along the east coast of Britain. Firing from static emplacements meant that the missile could be bigger and thus several features of its controls and flight system differed from the Thunderbird. The appearance was similar, a winged rocket carrying four booster motors, but instead of an internal solid fuel motor it had two ramjet sustainer motors on the exterior of the missile, the interior being used for fuel storage and supply. Guidance was by semi-active homing, the missile being directed to the vicinity of the target and then homing by detecting the radar signals emitted by a ground Target Illuminating Radar and reflected from the target.

SPECIFICATIONS
COUNTRY OF ORIGIN: United Kingdom
TYPE: Air Defense missiles
LENGTH: 27 feet 9 inches (8.46 m)
MAXIMUM SLANT RANGE: In excess of 50 miles (80 km)
WINGSPAN: 9 feet 3 inches (2.83 m)
WARHEAD: HE continuous rod; proximity fused
LAUNCH WEIGHT: not disclosed
DIAMETER: 27.5 inches (546 mm)

BM-21

The Soviet 122 mm BM-21 system was developed in the early 1950s and might be considered to be the successor to the various wartime "Katyusha" rocket systems, since it uses the same principle of firing a solid-fuel rocket from a bank of launchers mounted on the cargo bed of a 6x6 truck. Instead of the old open rails, however, this uses closed tubes in a cluster of 40 barrels, on a frame capable of 55° of elevation and 120° of traverse to either side. There are also 12- and 36- round variants of the basic launcher mounted on different vehicles. The rocket can be used with HE-Fragmentation, incendiary or bomblet warheads, and the rocket has four spring-put fins set at a slight angle in order to give the rocket a slow roll to stabilize it.

SPECIFICATIONS

COUNTRY OF ORIGIN: USSR
TYPE: Free-flight rockets
CALIBER: 122 mm
MAXIMUM RANGE: 12.66 miles (20.380 m)
MAXIMUM VELOCITY: 2264 feet/second (690 m/sec)
WEIGHT OF ROCKET: 170.85 pounds (77.5 kg)
LENGTH OF ROCKET: 10.58 feet (3.226 m)
LAUNCHER WEIGHT: 13.48 tons (13,700 kg), loaded
WARHEAD: HE-Fragmentation, incendiary, bomblet; 42.76 pounds (19.4 kg)

BM-27

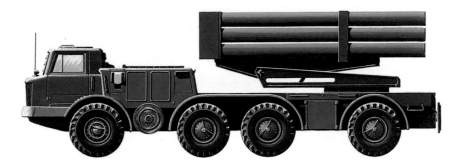

This Soviet 16-tube launcher appeared in the early 1970s and has collected a confusing series of names and numbers, from the M1977 to the most recent BM9P140. It consists of an 8x8 truck carrying a launch unit with two layers of four tubes and two layers of six tubes. This can be elevated to 55° and traversed 120° to either side of the vehicle. Four stabilizer jacks are lowered to provide support for the launcher while firing. The rocket is a solid-fuel type with a variety of warheads: HE-Fragmentation, chemical and sub-munition, the latter carrying either antitank/anti-personnel bomblets, incendiary bomblets, 24 anti-tank mines or 312 antipersonnel mines.

SPECIFICATIONS
COUNTRY OF ORIGIN: USSR
TYPE: Free-flight rockets
CALIBER: 220 mm
MAXIMUM RANGE: 15.5 miles (25,000 m)
MAXIMUM VELOCITY: not known
WEIGHT OF ROCKET: 573 pounds (260 kg)
LENGTH OF ROCKET: 15.85 feet (4.832 m)
LAUNCHER WEIGHT: 19,88 tons (20,000 kg)
WARHEAD: HE-Fragmentation; 220 pounds (100 kg)

CIS-40-AFL Grenade Launcher

This appeared in the late 1980s. one of several designs which came in the wake of the Russian AGS-17 but firing the American standard 40 mm grenade. A special longer-ranged cartridge was developed for these automatic weapons and this gives them a useful range, though like all such launchers it has a relatively flat trajectory and cannot "search" behind cover to flush out any lurking infantry in the same way that a mortar bomb can with its high trajectory. Nevertheless, as an anti-ambush weapon it has few equals, with its fast rate of fire giving it a lethal punch against unprotected infantry or light vehicles. Like the AGS-17, it became a common armament for light armored vehicles.

SPECIFICATIONS

COUNTRY OF ORIGIN: Singapore
TYPE: Light support weapons
CALIBER: 40 mm
MUZZLE VELOCITY: 791 feet/second (241 m/sec)
MAXIMUM RANGE: 2405 yards (2200 m)
LENGTH: 38.03 inches (966 mm)
WEIGHT: 72.75 pounds (33 kg)
RATE OF FIRE: 350 rds/min
WEIGHT OF PROJECTILE: 6.7 ounces (190 g)
FEED SYSTEM: disintegrating link belt, any convenient length
OPERATING SYSTEM: blowback, selective single shot or automatic fire

CSS-1

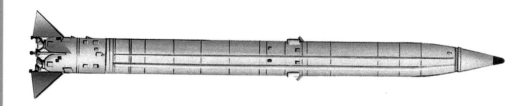

The Chinese CSS-1 was a single-stage, liquid-fueled, medium range ballistic missile generally similar to the Soviet SS-3 "Shyster" and probably built with some Soviet assistance. Called the T1 Tong Feng (East Wind) by the Chinese, it is variously claimed to have been put into service by 1966 or 1970 and was phased out during the late 1980s. Early versions are believed to have carried a simple 15kT warhead, but this was later replaced by a 25kT design and towards the end of their service most are understood to have been refitted with thermonuclear warheads. They were also used to maintain a useful threat against the Soviet Far Eastern territories.

SPECIFICATIONS
COUNTRY OF ORIGIN: China
TYPE: Surface-to-surface missiles
LENGTH: 68.8 feet (21 m)
RANGE: 1865 miles (3000 km)
WARHEAD: thermonuclear; 1.3 MT
PROPULSION: liquid fuel, single stage
GUIDANCE: inertial
LAUNCH WEIGHT: 26.57 tons (27,000 kg)
DIAMETER: 8.07 feet (2.46 m)

122 mm D-30

This all-round traverse howitzer was introduced into Soviet service in the early 1960s, and it is reasonable to assume that the designers took a close look at the Skoda leFH43 105 mm gun designed for the German army during World War II, since the D-30 employs a very similar system to obtain the desired 360° traverse. The trail of the gun splits into three legs which are then equi-spaced to provide a firm platform, above which the gun carriage can revolve. The folded legs lie beneath the barrel for traveling, and the gun muzzle has the towing connector attached to it, so that the length of the towed equipment is merely the length of the barrel. The D-30 has been adopted by numerous armies around the world.

SPECIFICATIONS

COUNTRY OF ORIGIN: USSR
TYPE: Field and heavy artillery
CALIBER: 122 mm
WEIGHT IN ACTION: 6945 pounds (3150 kg)
GUN LENGTH: 40 caliber: 16 feet (4.875 m)
ELEVATION: -7° to +70°
TRAVERSE: 360°
SHELL TYPE & WEIGHT: HE 47.97 pounds (21.761 kg)
MUZZLE VELOCITY: 2264 feet/second (690 m/sec)
MAXIMUM RANGE: 16,840 yards (15,400 m)

F

FIM-92 Stinger

The first shoulder-fired missile in service with the US Army was Redeye which could only work once the attack was over and the enemy was departing and showing a hot tail-pipe. Work began on a replacement in the early 1960s, the aim being an all-aspect system, and it was not until 1979 that production finally commenced. Stinger still uses an infra-red heat-seeking homer, but the principle has been refined and it now has an ultra-violet detector working in conjunction with the IR system to act as a sort of filter and make the system capable of homing on to any target except a head-on attacker (where the aircraft body conceals the exhaust plume). A limited IFF identification system is also incorporated in the latest version, as is the ability to be informed of approaching targets by any local radar network.

SPECIFICATIONS

COUNTRY OF ORIGIN: USA
TYPE: Air Defense missiles
LENGTH: 60 inches (1.52 m)
MAXIMUM SLANT RANGE: 3.1 miles (5000 m)
WINGSPAN: 3.58 inches (91 mm)
WARHEAD: HE-Frag; 6.6 pounds (3.0 kg); impact fused
LAUNCH WEIGHT: 22.25 pounds (10.1 kg)
DIAMETER: 2.75 inches (70 mm)

FROG-7

FROG stands for "Free Rocket Over Ground" and the Soviet FROG-1 rocket was first seen in 1957. FROG-7 appeared in 1969 after a series of improved models were developed as experience was gained. The system has been widely exported to several countries and the earlier -3, -4, -5, and -6 versions are probably still in use. FROG is a large single-stage solid fuel rocket provided with a variety of warheads and carried on an 8x8 transporter-erector-launcher vehicle. It is unusual in that it uses air-brakes in flight in order to alter the trajectory and thus achieve the desired range. The launch rail is elevated and the brake setting done before launch, according to the range desired. Like all fin-stabilized free rockets, crosswinds affect it and its accuracy is no better than a 546 yard (500 m) circle around the aiming point.

SPECIFICATIONS
COUNTRY OF ORIGIN: USSR
TYPE: Free-flight rockets
CALIBER: 550 mm
MAXIMUM RANGE: 43.5 miles (70 km)
MAXIMUM VELOCITY: not known
WEIGHT OF ROCKET: 5512 pounds (2500 kg)
LENGTH OF ROCKET: 29.88 feet (9.11 m)
LAUNCHER WEIGHT: 22.63 tons (23,000 kg)
WARHEAD: nuclear, 5 or 25 kT, chemical, HE; 992 pounds (450 kg)

G

Gepard

The Gepard self-propelled anti-aircraft gun system was designed specifically to protect armored formations. The system uses the hull of the Leopard 1 main battle tank to carry a welded-steel turret capable of powered traverse through 360° and accommodating the weapon system. The two 35mm cannon are located externally to avoid the problem of gun gas in the fighting compartment. Each of the weapons has a cyclic rate of fire of 550 rounds per minute, although it is standard procedure to fire bursts of between 20 and 40 rounds. Ammunition types include high explosive and armor-piercing. The fire-control system is based on a computer supplied with target data by two radars: the acquisition unit and the tracking unit. Other features are optical sights and a land navigation system.

SPECIFICATIONS

COUNTRY OF ORIGIN: Germany
TYPE: Self-propelled artillery
WEIGHT: 104,060 pounds (47,300 kg)
PERFORMANCE: maximum road speed 40.5 mph (65 km/h); fording 8 feet 2 inches (2.5 m); vertical obstacle 3 feet 9 inches (1.1 5 m); trench 9 feet 10 inches (3 m)
POWERPLANT: one MTU MB 838 Ca M500 10-cylinder multi-fuel engine developing 830 hp (619 kW)
ARMAMENT: two 35 mm cannon; eight smoke dischargers
ARMOR: 1.57 inches (40 mm)
DIMENSIONS: length: 25 feet 3 inches (7.68 m); width: 10 feet 9 inches (3.27 m); height: 9 feet 10 inches (3.01 m)
CREW: 4
RANGE: 342 miles (550 km)

GMLRS

The M30 GMLRS system was designed to increase the range and effectiveness of MLRS systems in service. The intention was to permit a smaller number of rockets to achieve the same effect as a large salvo of M26 MLRS rockets, decreasing the chance of collateral damage and reducing the logistics burden of rocket systems. GMLRS uses GPS guidance to increase the accuracy of its rockets, which can carry ether a single large (M31A1 Unitary) warhead or 404 bomblets in a Dual-Purpose Improved Conventional Munition (M30 DPICM). GMLRS rockets have more than twice the range of previous M26 rockets and have proven effective against targets in the rugged terrain of Afghanistan. While still not a "precision" weapon, GMLRS is accurate enough that frequently a single rocket will suffice where previously a large salvo would have been launched.

SPECIFICATIONS

COUNTRY OF ORIGIN: USA
TYPE: Free-flight rockets
CALIBER: 127 mm
MAXIMUM RANGE: 43.48 miles (70 km)
LENGTH: 22 feet 6.1 inches (6.86 m)
WEIGHT: 55,005 pounds (24,950 kg)
OPERATION: Inertial guidance with GPS
ROAD SPEED: 40 mph (64 km/h)
RANGE: 300 miles (483 km)
ENGINE TYPE: 500 hp Cummins diesel

155 mm Gun G-5

Unveiled at an exhibition in Athens in 1982, the 155 mm Gun G-5 astonished the rest of the world with its technical advances. It was, to some extent, based on the theories of Dr. Gerald Bull and adopted a special "extended range" projectile with stub wings. The remainder of the gun was fairly conventional, although it had auxiliary propulsion while most other people were still thinking about it. Using a split trail with four-wheeled bogie, the gun has a muzzle brake and a semi-automatic screw breech similar to that on the US M109 howitzer. The barrel swings over the trail for traveling, and a steerable wheel can be lowered from the train when the auxiliary motor is in use.

SPECIFICATIONS

COUNTRY OF ORIGIN: South Africa
TYPE: Field and heavy artillery
CALIBER: 155 mm
WEIGHT IN ACTION: 13.56 tons (13,750 kg)
GUN LENGTH: 45 caliber: 22.88 feet (6.975 m)
ELEVATION: -3° to +75°
TRAVERSE: 82°
SHELL TYPE & WEIGHT: HE 100 pounds (45.50 kg)
MUZZLE VELOCITY: 2942 feet/sec (897 m/sec)
MAXIMUM RANGE: 32,810 yards (30,000 m)

155 mm Howitzer FH-70

The 155 mm Howitzer FH-70 was a cooperative development between the United Kingdom, Germany, and Italy in 1968–74, one of the few such efforts which worked. The result was an advanced design, using an auxiliary power unit to provide self-propulsion for short distances, capable of firing a wide range of modern projectiles. It uses a split-trail carriage, the gun being swung over the trail legs for traveling, and provided with steerable wheels on the trail for self-movement. An efficient muzzle brake cuts down the recoil, and the vertical sliding block breech is used with combustible charges. In addition to the three original partners, the gun is also used by Japan, Saudi Arabia, and Malaysia. A self-propelled version, however, proved to be a technical disaster and was abandoned in 1986.

SPECIFICATIONS

COUNTRY OF ORIGIN: International (United Kingdom, Germany, and Italy)
TYPE: Field and heavy artillery
CALIBER: 155 mm
WEIGHT IN ACTION: 9.15 tons (9300 kg)
GUN LENGTH: 38 caliber: 19.75 feet (6.02 m)
ELEVATION: -4.5° to +70°
TRAVERSE: 56°
SHELL TYPE & WEIGHT: HE 95.90 pounds (43.5 kg)
MUZZLE VELOCITY: 2713 feet/second (827 m/sec)
MAXIMUM RANGE: 27,010 yards (24,700 m)

L

LGM-30F Minuteman 2

Minuteman was an American three-stage intercontinental ballistic missile carrying a single thermonuclear warhead. Minuteman 2 kept the same configuration but with increased range, increased payload, and a superior navigation system. The computer in the missile could now store a large number of alternative targets and the accuracy was greatly improved. Minuteman 3 appeared later and added a fourth stage with the adoption of a warhead containing three independently-targeted re-entry vehicles, each carrying a thermonuclear warhead. This version completely replaced Minuteman 2 in the 1980s. All Minuteman missiles were deployed in underground silos all over the continental United States, many being unmanned and remotely controlled.

SPECIFICATIONS
COUNTRY OF ORIGIN: USA
TYPE: Surface-to-surface missiles
LENGTH: 69.72 feet (18.2 m)
WINGSPAN: 8.53 feet (2.60 m)
RANGE: 1555 miles (2500 km)
WARHEAD: nuclear or HE; 1000 pounds (454 kg)
PROPULSION: solid fuel booster, turbofan sustainer engine
GUIDANCE: inertial, with terrain comparison
LAUNCH WEIGHT: 3181 pounds (1443 kg)
DIAMETER: 20 inches (530 mm)

105 mm Light Gun L118

The British used the Italian 105 mm Mod 56 for some years, but required something air-portable yet more powerful, and which, in addition, could fire the ammunition which had been developed for the Abbot SP gun. The 105 mm Light Gun L118 was the result, a lightweight gun using a tubular box trail and capable of firing in the howitzer role as well. It is provided with a second barrel, chambered for American 105 mm ammunition, so that if that ammunition is readily available in some distant theatre, then the gun is changed to suit, rather than requiring small quantities of Abbot ammunition to be hauled over long distances. It is helicopter-portable and has been used by Australia, New Zealand, India, the USA, and several Middle Eastern countries.

SPECIFICATIONS

COUNTRY OF ORIGIN: United Kingdom
TYPE: Field and heavy artillery
CALIBER: 105 mm
WEIGHT IN ACTION: 4100 pounds (1860 kg)
GUN LENGTH: 37 caliber: 12.72 feet (3.88 m)
ELEVATION: -5.5° to +70°
TRAVERSE: 11°
SHELL TYPE & WEIGHT: HE 35.38 pounds (16.05 kg)
MUZZLE VELOCITY: 2024 feet/second (617 m/sec)
MAXIMUM RANGE: 16,480 yards (15,070 m)

M

M109

The M109 was developed following a 1952 requirement for a self-propelled howitzer to replace the M44. The first production vehicles were completed in 1962 and survived numerous adaptations and upgrades to become the most widely used howitzer in the world, seeing action in Vietnam, in the Arab–Israeli Wars, and the Iran–Iraq War, and being exported to nearly 30 countries worldwide. It has an amphibious capability and fires a variety of projectiles including tactical nuclear shells. To date some 4000 are in use around the world, and the M109 has undergone numerous upgrades, including a new gun mount, new turret with longer barrel ordnance, automatic fire control, upgraded armor, and improved armor.

SPECIFICATIONS

COUNTRY OF ORIGIN: USA
TYPE: Self-propelled artillery
WEIGHT: 52,192 pounds (23,723 kg)
PERFORMANCE: maximum road speed 35 mph (56 km/h); fording 3 feet 6 inches (1.07 m); vertical obstacle 1 feet 9 inches (0.533 m); trench 6 feet (1.828 m)
POWERPLANT: one Detroit diesel Model 8V-71T diesel engine developing 405 hp (302 kW)
ARMAMENT: one 155 mm howitzer; one 12.7 mm anti-aircraft MG
ARMOR: classified
DIMENSIONS: 21 feet 8.25 inches (length 6.612 m); 10 feet 9.75 inches (width 3.295 m); height 10 feet 9.5 inches (3.289 m)
CREW: 6
RANGE: 240 miles (390 km)

M1974

After World War II the USSR concentrated development on towed artillery pieces, in contrast to NATO's drift towards self-propelled guns. It was not until 1974 that the first Soviet self-propelled howitzer made an appearance in public, hence its Western designation. Known as the Gvozdika in the USSR, the vehicle was deployed in large numbers (36 per tank division, 72 per motorized rifle division). Differing from the M1973 in being fully amphibious, the chassis has been used for a number of armored command and chemical warfare reconnaissance vehicles, as well as a mine-clearing vehicle. It can also be fitted with wider tracks to allow it to operate in snow or swamp conditions. The M1974 was widely exported to Soviet client states as well as Angola, Algeria, and Iraq.

SPECIFICATIONS

COUNTRY OF ORIGIN: USSR
TYPE: Self-propelled artillery
WEIGHT: 34,540 pounds (15,700 kg)
PERFORMANCE: maximum road speed 37 mph (60 km/h); fording amphibious; vertical obstacle 3 feet 7 inches (1.10 m); trench 9 feet 10 inches (3.00 m)
POWERPLANT: one YaMZ-238V V-8 water-cooled diesel engine developing 240 hp (179 kW)
ARMAMENT: one 122 mm gun; one 7.62 mm anti-aircraft MG
ARMOR: 0.59–0.78 inches (15–20 mm)
DIMENSIONS: length 23 feet 11.5 inches (7.30 m); width 9 feet 4 inches (2.85 m); height 7 feet 10.5 inches (2.40 m)
CREW: 4
RANGE: 310 miles (500 km)

M203 Grenade Launcher

The original US grenade-launching weapon was the M79, a single-shot gun carried by one of the infantry squad. This put the soldier at a disadvantage when he needed a rifle for self-defense, and therefore this M203 launcher was devised, a single-shot weapon which could be attached beneath the M16 rifle, so that the soldier had both rifle and launcher in one unit. The launcher is breech-loaded by sliding the barrel forward to expose the chamber and loading the round from beneath. The barrel slides back and locks, and behind it is the trigger and self-cocking firing mechanism. There is also a grenade-launching sight, making the M203 a totally separate item from the parent rifle. The grenade uses a low-power cartridge, in order to keep the recoil force down to a manageable level.

SPECIFICATIONS

COUNTRY OF ORIGIN: USA
TYPE: Light support weapons
CALIBER: 40 mm
MUZZLE VELOCITY: 246 feet/seconds (75 m/sec)
MAXIMUM RANGE: 437 yards (400 m)
LENGTH: 15 inches (380 mm)
WEIGHT: 3 pounds (1.36 kg)
RATE OF FIRE: 8–10 rds/min
WEIGHT OF PROJECTILE: 6.7 ounces (190 g)
FEED SYSTEM: Single shot, hand-loaded
OPERATING SYSTEM: single-shot, self-cocking

MIM-104 Patriot

Patriot is the anti-missile missile, and its formidable specification took close to 20 years of study and development before it was allowed into service. It finally got the chance to display its power during the Gulf War, countering the Iraqi Scuds being fired towards Israel, but argument still rages about whether they were effective or not. The Patriot missile has a high-efficiency 11.5 second solid fuel rocket motor. A surveillance radar detects a target and informs the missile of its general direction, so that it will turn towards the target after launch and thus be gathered by a tracking radar. This guides it to the area of the target where an on-board radar takes charge and homes the missile on to the target. A proximity fuse then detonates the warhead when within lethal distance.

SPECIFICATIONS
COUNTRY OF ORIGIN: USA
TYPE: Air Defense missiles
LENGTH: 17 feet (5.18 m)
MAXIMUM SLANT RANGE: 100 miles (160 km)
WINGSPAN: 36 inches (920 mm)
WARHEAD: HE-Frag; 160 pounds (73 kg); proximity fused
LAUNCH WEIGHT: 1545 pounds (700 kg)
DIAMETER: 16.15 inches (410 mm)

M

MIM-23 HAWK

HAWK means "Homing All-the-Way Killer" and is a surprisingly long-lived US system which began development in 1952 and was used by the US until 2002. It was designed to be a low-level system for deployment with field armies. Although cumbersome and needing large numbers of soldiers and vehicles, it was accepted because nothing else was remotely as good, and with a few modifications it has remained perfectly serviceable. The missile has a two-stage solid fuel motor, giving both an initial high acceleration rate and sustained thrust. The original launcher was a three-missile cluster on a trailer but fixed and mobile launchers with up to nine missiles are now in use. The Hawk is a radar homer which picks up signals from a radar which are reflected by the target, and steers itself to interception.

SPECIFICATIONS
COUNTRY OF ORIGIN: USA
TYPE: Air Defense missiles
LENGTH: 16.8 feet (5.12 m)
MAXIMUM SLANT RANGE: 25 miles (40 km)
WINGSPAN: 3.95 feet (1.206 m)
WARHEAD: HE continuous rod; 120 pounds (54.4 kg); impact and proximity fused
LAUNCH WEIGHT: 1380 pounds (626 kg)
DIAMETER: 14.5 inches (370 mm)

MLRS

The Vought Multiple Launch Rocket System (MLRS) had its origins in a 1976 feasibility study into what was known as a General Support Rocket System. Following trials, the Vought system was chosen and entered service with the US Army in 1982. These Self-Propelled Launcher Loaders on the chassis of the M2 Infantry Fighting Vehicle carry two pods of six rounds each. These rounds might consist of fragmentation bomblets, anti-tank mines, chemical warheads, or mine-dispensing munitions. The Vought MLRS was licensed to the UK, France, Italy, West Germany, and the Netherlands for production. It saw action during the 1991 Gulf War, when Allied MLRS batteries tore large holes in Iraqi defense lines prior to the ground offensive to free Kuwait.

SPECIFICATIONS

COUNTRY OF ORIGIN: USA
TYPE: Free-flight rockets
CALIBER: 227 mm
MAXIMUM RANGE: 26.1 miles (42 km)
MAXIMUM VELOCITY: not known
WEIGHT OF ROCKET: 679 pounds (308 kg)
LENGTH OF ROCKET: 12.93 feet (3.94 m)
LAUNCHER WEIGHT: 55,420 pounds (25,191 kg)
WARHEAD: submunition; chemical; weights not known

Nike Hercules

Nike Hercules was the second generation of Nike and it was an attempt to produce a system which was more efficient, but at the same time simpler to use. It also had to be compatible with Nike Ajax and use as much of that expensive system as possible. The missile itself was vastly improved, with a speed of Mach 3.5 and the ability to intercept a target at altitudes of well over 25 miles (40,000 m), and it destroyed the idea, still lingering in the minds of aviators, that missiles could be evaded by flying high and fast. The system was deployed in the US by late 1958 and in subsequent years it was supplied to several countries in order to upgrade their earlier Nike Ajax versions.

SPECIFICATIONS
COUNTRY OF ORIGIN: USA
TYPE: Air Defense missiles
LENGTH: 41 feet (12.5 m)
MAXIMUM SLANT RANGE: 96 miles (155 km)
WINGSPAN: 74 inches (1.88 m)
WARHEAD: HE; 1108 pounds (503 kg) or nuclear
LAUNCH WEIGHT: 10,405 pounds (4720 kg)
DIAMETER: 31.5 inches (800 mm)

OTO-Melara 105 mm Mod 56

The OTO-Melara 105 mm Mod 56 was developed in the 1950s to meet a demand from many countries for a 105 mm howitzer capable of firing the standard US M1 family of ammunition and yet light enough to be lifted by the helicopters of the time. This weapon is a pack howitzer, capable of being dismantled into 12 pack loads, and the suspension system allows the weapon to be set high, leaving room for the breech to recoil at high angles of elevation, or low for flat-trajectory firing against tanks and similar targets. As such it was a highly flexible gun and was widely adopted throughout NATO in the 1950s.

SPECIFICATIONS

COUNTRY OF ORIGIN: Italy
TYPE: Field and heavy artillery
CALIBER: 105 mm
WEIGHT IN ACTION: 2806 pounds (1273 kg)
GUN LENGTH: 14 caliber: 57.9 inches (1.47 m)
ELEVATION: -7° to +65°
TRAVERSE: 56°
SHELL TYPE & WEIGHT: HE 33.0 pounds (14.97 kg)
MUZZLE VELOCITY: 1345 feet/seconds (416 m/sec)
MAXIMUM RANGE: 12,140 yards (11,100 m)

Panzerhaubitze 2000

As a result of the collapse of the tri-national SP70 project, Germany had to find a new SP howitzer. Designs were solicited from two companies, and after examination, the one offered by Wegmann/ MaK was accepted and contracts were issued. It was first used in combat in 2006, in Afghanistan. The hull and running gear are based on those of the Leopard II tank, but with the engine and transmission at the front of the hull. The rear is surmounted by a large turret containing the 52-caliber length gun which has a sliding block breech and a large multi-baffle muzzle-brake. The gun and turret are entirely power-operated and there is an automatic mechanical loading system which permits the firing of three rounds in ten seconds.

SPECIFICATIONS

COUNTRY OF ORIGIN: Germany
TYPE: Self-propelled artillery
WEIGHT: 54.13 tons (55,000 kg)
PERFORMANCE: maximum road speed 27 mph (60 km/h); fording 7 feet 5 inches (2.25 m); vertical obstacle 3 feet 3 inches (1 m); trench 9 feet 10 inches (3 m)
POWERPLANT: one MTU 881 V-12 diesel developing 745.7 kW (1000 hp)
ARMAMENT: one 155 mm howitzer
ARMOR: not disclosed
DIMENSIONS: length 25 feet 10 inches (7.87 m); width 11 feet (3.37 m); height 11 feet 2 inches (3.4 m)
CREW: 5
RANGE: 260 miles (420 km)

Pershing

Pershing was a tactical battlefield support system, transportable in various large cargo aircraft. Originally mounted on tracked chassis, the Pershing 1A system moved towards the use of wheeled vehicles. This system also improved the programming of the missile with target information and introduced an automatic count-down system. Pershing 2 appeared in the mid-1980s with an entirely new navigation system and a new re-entry vehicle warhead incorporating a highly accurate terminal guidance system. The range was also increased by about 1125 miles (1800 km), bringing Moscow into range for those Pershings based in Germany. The basic missile was a two-stage solid fuel weapon with a nuclear warhead.

SPECIFICATIONS

COUNTRY OF ORIGIN: USA
TYPE: Surface-to-surface missiles
LENGTH: 34 feet 10 inches (10.61 m)
RANGE: 5000+ miles (8000+ km)
WARHEAD: ten 500 kT MIRV
PROPULSION: solid/liquid, four-stage
GUIDANCE: inertial
LAUNCH WEIGHT: 87 tons (88,450 kg)
DIAMETER: 7.67 feet (2.34 m)

Rascal Light 155mm SP Howitzer

The "Rascal" was a private venture by Soltam, the Israel manufacturers, and represents an entirely new design of SP gun. The object was to produce a gun that was light enough not to be restricted by the carrying capacity of rural bridges, and able to be air-lifted. The vehicle is not based upon any existing tank; the hull has a raised driver's compartment at the left front, with the engine behind the driver, and a central compartment for the commander and two gunners. The 155 mm howitzer is installed on a platform at the rear of the vehicle and is power-operated; the gun may be either 39- or 52-calibers in length. A total of 40 rounds of ammunition are carried; the shells in racks alongside the gun, and the cartridges in an armor-protected compartment in the hull.

SPECIFICATIONS

COUNTRY OF ORIGIN: Israel
TYPE: Self-propelled artillery
WEIGHT: 19,500 kg (10.19 tons)
PERFORMANCE: maximum road speed 30 mph (48 km/h)
POWERPLANT: one diesel developing 350 hp (260.9 kW)
ARMAMENT: one 155 mm howitzer
ARMOR: not disclosed
DIMENSIONS: length 24 feet 7 inches (7.50 m); width 8 feet 1 inches (2.46 m); height: 7 feet 6 inches (2.30 m)
CREW: 4
RANGE: 218 miles (350 km)

SA-1 Guild

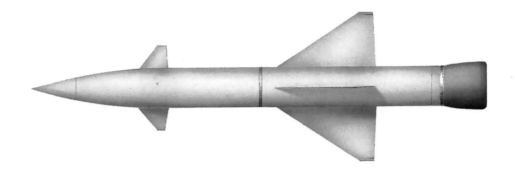

The Soviet SA-1 Guild went into service in the mid-1950s and remained in first-line units until the early 1980s. The design was based upon the German wartime "Wasserfall" missile, development of which was still in progress when the war ended in 1945. The result was a liquid-fuel rocket motor fed by turbine pumps and controlled in flight by fins and canards. The target is detected by an acquisition radar and passed to a tracking radar which locks on. The missile is steered into the beam and kept there by radio control until its proximity fuse detects the target and detonates the warhead. The missile went through several degrees of modification during its service life, suggesting that the initial design was not particularly good, and it is known that many were fired at US spy planes without success.

SPECIFICATIONS

COUNTRY OF ORIGIN: USSR
TYPE: Air Defense missiles
LENGTH: 39 feet 4 inches (12 m)
MAXIMUM SLANT RANGE: 24.8 miles (40 km)
WINGSPAN: 8 feet 10 inches (2.70 m)
WARHEAD: HE-Frag; 551 pounds (250 kg); impact and proximity fuses
LAUNCH WEIGHT: 7716 pounds (3500 kg)
DIAMETER: 27.5 inches (70 mm)

SA-10 Grumble

The S-300PMU1 (NATO reporting name SA-10 Grumble) is a cutting-edge air-defense system developed in the early 1970s, operational service beginning in 1980. The key advantage of the SA-10 is that it can acquire and engage multiple targets simultaneously across a very broad spectrum of altitude – 82 feet (25 m) to 98,400 feet (30,000 m). The four-missile erector-launcher is mounted on a 5P85SE2 or 5P85TE2 semi-trailer pulled by a MAZ-7910 8x8 tractor truck. Three missiles can be launched in one second, each for different targets. During deployment, the missile battery consists of an engagement control center, a Doppler target-acquisition radar, a trailer-mounted FLAP LID radar system, and up to 12 erector launchers.

SPECIFICATIONS

COUNTRY OF ORIGIN: USSR/Russia
TYPE: Anti-Aircraft Vehicles
CREW: Unknown
WEIGHT: 95,500 pounds (43,300 kg)
DIMENSIONS: Length: 37.63 feet (11.47 m); width: 33.36 feet (10.17 m); height: 12.14 feet (3.7 m)
RANGE: 400 miles (650 km)
ARMOR: Classified
ARMAMENT: 4 x 5V55K SA-10 SAMs
POWERPLANT: 1 x D12A-525A 12-cylinder diesel, developing 517 hp (386 kW)
PERFORMANCE: Maximum road speed: 37 mph (60 km/h)

SA-7 Grail

This shoulder-fired missile has been exported all over the world to legitimate armies, irregular forces, freedom fighters, and terrorists of every political shade. It was probably copied from the American Redeye and has similar shortcomings, but as a hand-held weapon it is a reasonable performer. The firer, on seeing a target, merely has to shoulder the weapon, aim and press a firing switch. This turns on the heat-seeking head of the missile which, as soon as it acquires the target, gives a signal, and the firer then presses the trigger and the missile is launched. It steers itself towards the target but can be distracted by anything producing more heat and is easily fooled by pyrotechnic counter-measures.

SPECIFICATIONS
COUNTRY OF ORIGIN: USSR
TYPE: Air Defense missiles
LENGTH: 53.25 inches (1.25 m)
MISSILE WEIGHT: 20.3 pounds (9.2 kg)
LAUNCHER WEIGHT: 9.20 pounds (4.17 kg)
MAXIMUM SLANT RANGE: 6 miles (10 km)
WARHEAD: HE-Frag; 2.53 pounds (1.15 kg); impact fused
DIAMETER: 2.75 inches (70 mm)

SMAW

SMAW (Shoulder-fired Multi-purpose Assault Weapon) is a portable rocket launcher with a variety of warhead options to use against different target types. It resembles the Israeli B-300 or the earlier French LRAC in that it consists of two parts, the launch tube with sights and aiming rifle, and the disposable rocket container which locks on to the back of the launch tube and is discarded after the rocket has been fired. The spotting rifle fires a special 9mm explosive bullet which is matched to the rocket. The soldier fires the rifle until he gets a hit, then holds the same aim and fires the rocket. The basic warhead is HE Dual Purpose which can be used against light armor or hard fortifications, and there is also a specialized HEAA anti-armor warhead capable of defeating main battle tanks.

SPECIFICATIONS
COUNTRY OF ORIGIN: USA
TYPE: Light support weapons
CALIBER: 3.26 inches (83 mm)
WEIGHT: 16.5 pounds (7.5 kg)
WEIGHT OF HEAA: 14.1 pounds (6.4 kg)
WEIGHT OF HEDP: 13.1 pounds (5.950 kg)
LENGTH AS FIRED: 54.25 inches (1.378 m)
LENGTH OF LAUNCHER: 32.5 inches (825 mm)
LAUNCH VELOCITY: 721 feet/second (220 m/sec)

Soltam M68 Gun

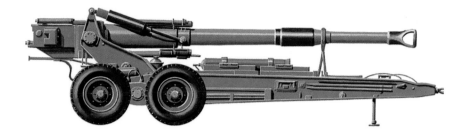

A development of a Finnish design, the Israeli M68 is a split-trail gun-howitzer of reasonable weight and good performance. The carriage has two wheels at the forward end of each trail leg, so that they move with the legs as they are opened. There are loose spades which are driven into the ground and then have the trail locked to them by wedges. The gun had an efficient muzzle brake and a fume extractor, indicating the use of the same gun in a self-propelled carriage. For movement, the top carriage revolves until the barrel is above the folded trail legs, where it is then locked, and the trail ends are hoisted up and hooked to the towing truck. An unusual feature is the use of a sliding block breech with bag charges, the breech block having a sealing ring inset in its front face.

SPECIFICATIONS

COUNTRY OF ORIGIN: Israel
TYPE: Field and heavy artillery
CALIBER: 155 mm
WEIGHT IN ACTION: 9.35 tons (9500 kg)
GUN LENGTH: 32 caliber: 17 feet (5.18 m)
ELEVATION: -10° to +52°
TRAVERSE: 90°
SHELL TYPE & WEIGHT: HE 96.34 pounds (43.700 kg)
MUZZLE VELOCITY: 2690 feet/second (820 m/sec)
MAXIMUM RANGE: 25,700 yards (23,500 m)

SS-1 Scud B

The original SS-1 Scud missile was, like the US "Corporal" of the same era, little more than an improved German V2 missile needing to be fueled after erection and taking its time about deployment. This did not fit Soviet tactical thinking and Scud-B appeared in the mid-1960s. This used a faster and lighter transporter-erector-launcher vehicle based on an 8x8 wheeled chassis, modernized the erecting and positioning mechanisms, and replaced the old radio-controlled fuel-cutoff and ballistic trajectory form of near-guidance with an up-to-date inertial system. All of this technology produced a weapon which could get to its firing site and engage its missile much quicker than the original. The Scud was supplied to Warsaw Pact armies and also to many Middle Eastern countries, where improved versions are still to be found.

SPECIFICATIONS

COUNTRY OF ORIGIN: USSR
TYPE: Surface-to-surface missiles
LENGTH: 36 feet 11 inches (11.25 m)
RANGE: 555 miles (900 km)
WARHEAD: nuclear
PROPULSION: liquid, single stage
GUIDANCE: inertial
LAUNCH WEIGHT: 9.55 tons (9700 kg)
DIAMETER: 39.37 inches (1.0 m)

SS-9 Scarp

This monstrous machine was once described as the largest mass-produced weapon ever made, a description it is difficult to argue with. Deployed in huge underground silos in the mid-1960s, some of its test shots, monitored by radar by the US, displayed such range and accuracy that the West really began to worry about Soviet capabilities and intentions. The design continued to advance in complexity, the first models having a warhead of about 20MT, the second 25MT, the third was designed for low-level flight to avoid radars, and the fourth went to multiple warheads. Finally, Model 5 went into orbit with a satellite-destroying capability. By the late 1970s over 300 were deployed, but in the 1980s they were removed, to be replaced by an even bigger weapon, the SS-18.

SPECIFICATIONS

COUNTRY OF ORIGIN: USSR
TYPE: Surface-to-surface missiles
LENGTH: 118 feet (36.0 m)
RANGE: 4970 miles (8000 km)
WARHEAD: nuclear; 600 kT
PROPULSION: solid, three stage
GUIDANCE: inertial
LAUNCH WEIGHT: 33.46 tons (34,000 kg)
DIAMETER: 5.57 feet (1.7 m)

Titan

When Atlas, the first American intercontinental ballistic missile, was created, it was considered wise to start up a second line of development in case Atlas failed; this Atlas 2 was re-named Titan, and eventually became an ICBM in its own right. Titan was created some time after Atlas and therefore was the receptacle for many ideas which had arisen after seeing the result of earlier ideas put into practice on Atlas. But in the same way, some ideas dreamed up for Titan — such as the inertial guidance system — were used for Atlas and Titan ended up with other alternatives. Nevertheless, the result was a sound and serviceable missile, about 50 of which were sunk into silos across the US. Titan 2 was new from tip to tail and was designed to use storable liquid fuel and be permanently ready for immediate launch.

SPECIFICATIONS

COUNTRY OF ORIGIN: USA
TYPE: Surface-to-surface missiles
LENGTH: 98 feet (29.9 m)
RANGE: 7770 miles (12,500 km)
WARHEAD: thermonuclear, 2 MT
PROPULSION: solid fuel, three-stage
GUIDANCE: inertial
LAUNCH WEIGHT: 31.24 tons (31,746 kg)
DIAMETER: 72.4 inches (1.84 m)

TOS-1

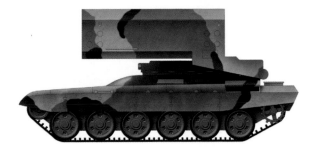

Based on the chassis of the T-72 main battle tank, the TOS-1 Multiple Rocket Launcher delivers a fuel-air warhead. A fine mist of flammable vapor is formed when the warhead detonates, and is then ignited to create an intense thermobaric effect. The timing of ignition has to be extremely precise; if not the weapon will produce an impressive amount of flame but not the intended massive pressure wave. Fuel-air systems of this sort can be used to clear mines or as an area effect weapon against heavily fortified troops. Also known as "Buratino", the TOS-1 system was first tested in Afghanistan in the 1980s and was probably used to clear booby traps and mines (and enemy personnel) in Grozny during conflicts in Chechnya. The launcher vehicle can deliver its entire load of 30 rockets in about 15 seconds.

SPECIFICATIONS

COUNTRY OF ORIGIN: Russia/Soviet Union
TYPE: Free-flight rockets
CALIBER: 8.7 inches (220 mm)
SHELL TYPE & WEIGHT: 220 mm rocket with thermobaric or high explosive warhead
MAXIMUM RANGE: 2.17-2.48 miles (3.5-4 km)
LENGTH: 31 feet 3.2 inches (9.53 m)
WEIGHT: 92,594 pounds (42,000 kg)
OPERATION: Not known
ROAD SPEED: 37.3 miles (60 km/h);
RANGE: 342 miles (550 km);
ENGINE TYPE: 840 hp diesel

Type: 63

To meet their needs for a self-propelled anti-aircraft gun, the Chinese took the chassis of the Soviet T-34 tank (supplied to them in large numbers by the USSR) and added an open-topped turret with twin anti-aircraft guns. The resulting vehicle, the Type: 63, was severely limited in that it had no provision for radar control and had to be sighted and elevated manually, a major drawback when faced with fast, low-flying aircraft, particularly as the gun had to be loaded manually with five-round clips. It was supplied to the Viet Cong during the Vietnam War in the 1960s, but otherwise was only used in small numbers by the People's Liberation Army. Amazingly, given its mediocre qualities, it continued to be used by the Chinese until the late 1980s.

SPECIFICATIONS

COUNTRY OF ORIGIN: China
TYPE: Self-propelled artillery
WEIGHT: 32,000 kg (70,400 pounds)
PERFORMANCE: maximum road speed 34 mph (55 km/h); fording 4 feet 4 inches (1.32 m); vertical obstacle 2 feet 5 inches (0.73 m); trench 8 feet 2 inches (2.5 m)
POWERPLANT: one V-12 water-cooled diesel engine developing 500 hp (373 kW)
ARMAMENT: twin 37 mm anti-aircraft cannon
ARMOR: 0.7-1.8 inches (18-45 mm)
DIMENSIONS: length 21 feet 1 inches (6.432 m); width 9 feet 10 inches (2.99 m); height 9 feet 10 inches (2.995 m)
CREW: 6
RANGE: 186 miles (300 km)

ZSU-23-490 mm M1

The ZSU-23-4 was developed in the 1960s as the replacement for the ZSU-57-2. Although it had a shorter firing range, the radar fire-control and an increased firing rate made the weapon much more effective. The chassis was similar to that of the SA-6 surface-to-air missile (SAM) system and used components of the PT-76 tank. Known to the Soviets as the "Shilka", the vehicle can create an impassable wall of anti-aircraft fire over an 180° arc. Widely exported, the ZSU-23-4 was particularly effective in Egyptian hands during the Yom Kippur War of 1973, bringing down Israeli aircraft who were forced to fly low by the Egyptian missile defense system. It also saw extensive combat service with the North Vietnamese during the Vietnam War, bringing down numerous American aircraft.

SPECIFICATIONS

COUNTRY OF ORIGIN: USSR
TYPE: Self-propelled artillery
WEIGHT: 41,800 pounds (19,000 kg)
PERFORMANCE: maximum road speed 27 mph (44 km/h); fording 4 feet 7 inches (1.4 m); vertical obstacle 3 feet 7 inches (1.10 m); trench 9 feet 2 inches (2.80 m)
POWERPLANT: one V-6R diesel engine developing 280 hp (210 kW)
ARMAMENT: four AZP-23 23mm anti-aircraft cannon
ARMOR: 0.39-0.6 inches (10-15 mm)
DIMENSIONS: length 21 feet 5 inches (6.54 m); width 9 feet 8 inches (2.95m); height (without radar) 7 feet 4 inches (2.25 m)
CREW: 4
RANGE: 162 miles (260 km)

ARTILLERY

1945 TO TODAY

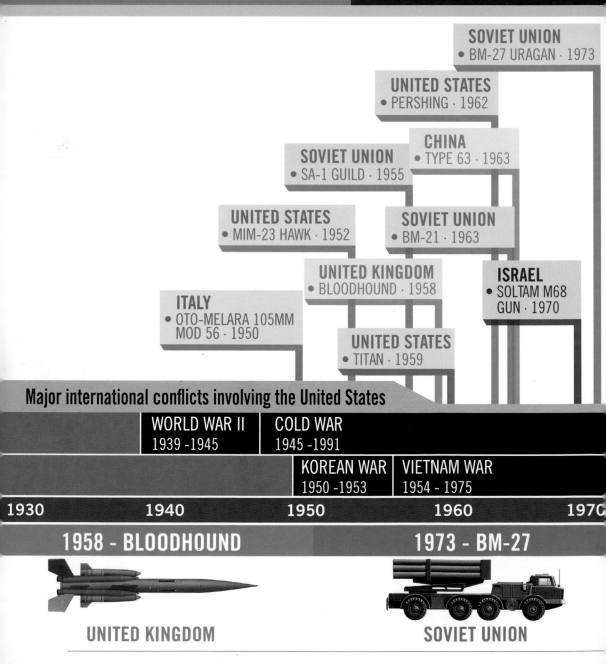

SOVIET UNION
- BM-27 URAGAN · 1973

UNITED STATES
- PERSHING · 1962

CHINA
- TYPE 63 · 1963

SOVIET UNION
- SA-1 GUILD · 1955

UNITED STATES
- MIM-23 HAWK · 1952

SOVIET UNION
- BM-21 · 1963

UNITED KINGDOM
- BLOODHOUND · 1958

ISRAEL
- SOLTAM M68 GUN · 1970

ITALY
- OTO-MELARA 105MM MOD 56 · 1950

UNITED STATES
- TITAN · 1959

Major international conflicts involving the United States

WORLD WAR II 1939 -1945	COLD WAR 1945 -1991	
	KOREAN WAR 1950 -1953	VIETNAM WAR 1954 - 1975

| 1930 | 1940 | 1950 | 1960 | 1970 |

1958 - BLOODHOUND

1973 - BM-27

UNITED KINGDOM

SOVIET UNION

FEATURED WEAPONS TIMELINE

This timeline features notable advancements in military technologies by influential nations worldwide.

SINGAPORE
- CIS-40-AFL GRENADE LAUNCHER · 1987

SOVIET UNION
- TOS-1 · 1988

UNITED STATES
- MIM-104 PATRIOT · 1981

UNITED STATES
- SMAW · 1984

UNITED KINGDOM
- AS-90 · 1993

UNITED STATES
- GMLRS · 2007

GERMANY
GEPARD · 1976

ISRAEL
- RASCAL LIGHT 155MM SP HOWITZER · 1990

GERMANY
- PANZERHAUBITZE 2000 · 2006

UNITED STATES
- RAW (RIFLEMAN'S ASSAULT WEAPON) · 1990

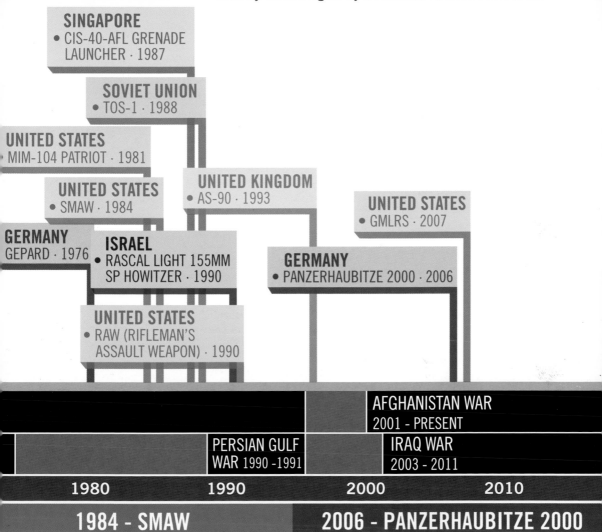

AFGHANISTAN WAR
2001 - PRESENT

PERSIAN GULF WAR 1990 -1991

IRAQ WAR
2003 - 2011

| 1980 | 1990 | 2000 | 2010 |

1984 - SMAW

2006 - PANZERHAUBITZE 2000

UNITED STATES

GERMANY

Glossary

anti-tank projectiles
a powerful, explosive warhead that can pierce through armor

armament
the weapons, supplies, and soldiers used by a military force

camouflage
an inconsistent pattern of colors and shapes that blends in with the surroundings

collateral damage
death, injuries, or damage on something other than the intended target

counter-battery operation
locating and firing upon enemy artillery

countermeasure
an action or device that negates or offset another action or device

diplomacy
working to maintain relations between the government of other countries

field-glasses
binoculars

flechette projectiles
a small dart-shaped projectile clustered within an explosive warhead

gyro compass
a navigational compass that always points to the geographic north

Hezbollah
an organization of militant Shiite Muslims based in Lebanon and engaged in guerrilla warfare against Israel

howitzer
a short cannon used to fire projectiles at medium muzzle velocities and with relatively high trajectories

infrared
of or relating to the range of invisible radiation wavelengths

logarithms
used in mathematical calculations to depict the perceived levels of variable quantities such as visible light energy, electromagnetic field strength, and sound

marshalling yards
a place where equipment is kept and organized for military operations

nonrecoil
something that does not spring back

nuclear warheads
an explosive weapon that derives its destructive force from a nuclear reaction

projectile
something such as a bullet or rocket that is thrown or driven forward as a weapon

propellant chemistry
the combination of fuel and an oxidizing agent to create gases that can produce thrust

repercussions
the unexpected effect of something said or done

SMART system
an acronym for Self-Monitoring Analysis and Report Technology, which is a system designed to analyze itself to find problems that may occur and then take corrective action

stratosphere
the upper portion of the atmosphere where the temperature changes little and clouds rarely form

watershed
a time when an important change occurs

Further Information

Websites

http://www.militaryhistoryonline.com/wwii/usarmy/artillery.aspx
An in-depth look at the artillery used by the US Army in World War II.

http://www.cr.nps.gov/history/online_books/source/is3/is3toc.htm
Illustrative history of artillery, presented by the National Park Service.

http://www.hulu.com/watch/393693
21st century war machines.

http://www.strategypage.com/dls/articles/21st-Century-War-How-It-Will-Be-Different-And-Why-2-3-2014.asp
Discusses new trends in warfare.

Books

Bishop, Chris. *The Encyclopedia of Weapons: From World War II to the Present Day.* Thunder Bay Press, 2006.
A compilation of various types of weapons used by militaries.

Norris, John. *Artillery: A History.* The History Press, 2012.
An overview of the development of artillery throughout history.

Shank, Carol. *U.S. Military Weapons and Artillery.* Capstone Press, 2012.
A review of weapons and artillery used by the US military.

Zaloga, Steven J. *US Field Artillery of World War II.* Osprey Publishing, Limited, 2007.
Discusses the artillery used by the US during WWII, and how it differed from previous wars.

Index of Artillery Profile Pages